discard

Professional Athlete
& Sports Official

Career Assessments & Their Meaning
Childcare Worker
Clergy
Computer Programmer
Financial Advisor
Firefighter
Homeland Security Officer
Journalist
Manager
Military & Elite Forces Officer
Nurse
Politician
Professional Athlete & Sports Official
Psychologist
Research Scientist
Social Worker
Special Education Teacher
Veterinarian

CAREERS WITH CHARACTER

Professional Athlete & Sports Official

Joyce Libal and Rae Simons

Mason Crest

Mason Crest
450 Parkway Drive, Suite D
Broomall, PA 19008
www.masoncrest.com

Printed in the USA.

First printing
9 8 7 6 5 4 3 2

Series ISBN: 978-1-4222-2750-3
ISBN: 978-1-4222-2763-3
ebook ISBN: 978-1-4222-9059-0

Cataloging-in-Publication Data on file with the Library of Congress.

Produced by Vestal Creative Services.
www.vestalcreative.com

Photo Credits:
Comstock: p. 22
Corbis: pp. 10, 12, 15, 16, 18, 24, 25, 26, 27, 32, 34, 36, 37, 38, 39, 42, 44, 45, 47, 50, 52, 53, 55, 58, 60, 68, 69, 70, 74, 77, 85, 86, 88
PhotoDisc: p. 29
Reuters: pp. 62

The individuals in these images are models, and the images are for illustrative purposes only. To the best knowledge of the publisher, all other images are in the public domain. If any image has been inadvertently uncredited or miscredited, please notify Vestal Creative Services, Vestal, New York 13850, so that rectification can be made for future printings.

CONTENTS

We each leave a fingerprint on the world.
Our careers are the work we do in life.
Our characters are shaped by the choices
we make to do good.
When we combine careers with character,
we touch the world with power.

INTRODUCTION

by Dr. Cheryl Gholar
and Dr. Ernestine G. Riggs

In today's world, the awesome task of choosing or staying in a career has become more involved than one would ever have imagined in past decades. Whether the job market is robust or the demand for workers is sluggish, the need for top-performing employees with good character remains a priority on most employers' lists of "must have" or "must keep." When critical decisions are being made regarding a company or organization's growth or future, job performance and work ethic are often the determining factors as to who will remain employed and who will not.

How does one achieve success in one's career and in life? Victor Frankl, the Austrian psychologist, summarized the concept of success in the preface to his book *Man's Search for Meaning* as: "The unintended side-effect of one's personal dedication to a course greater than oneself." Achieving value by responding to life and careers from higher levels of knowing and being is a specific goal of teaching and learning in "Careers with Character." What constitutes success for us as individuals can be found deep within our belief system. Seeking, preparing, and attaining an excellent career that aligns with our personality is an outstanding goal. However, an excellent career augmented by exemplary character is a visible expression of the human need to bring meaning, purpose, and value to our work.

Career education informs us of employment opportunities, occupational outlooks, earnings, and preparation needed to perform certain tasks. Character education provides insight into how a person of good character might choose to respond, initiate an action, or perform specific tasks in the presence of an ethical dilemma. "Careers with Character" combines the two and teaches students that careers are more than just jobs. Career development is incomplete without character development. What better way to explore careers and character than to make them a single package to be opened, examined, and reflected upon as a means of understanding the greater whole of who we are and what work can mean when one chooses to become an employee of character?

Character can be defined simply as "who you are even when no one else is around." Your character is revealed by your choices and actions. These bear your personal signature, validating the story of who you are. They are the fingerprints you leave behind on the people you meet and know; they are the ideas you bring into reality. Your choices tell the world what you truly believe.

Character, when viewed as a standard of excellence, reminds us to ask ourselves when choosing a career: "Why this particular career, for what purpose, and to what end?" The authors of "Careers with Character" knowledgeably and passionately, through their various vignettes, enable one to experience an inner journey that is both intellectual and moral. Students will find themselves, when confronting decisions in real life, more prepared, having had experiential learning opportunities through this series. The books, however, do not separate or negate the individual good from the academic skills or intellect needed to perform the required tasks that lead to productive career development and personal fulfillment.

Each book is replete with exemplary role models, practical strategies, instructional tools, and applications. In each volume, individuals of character work toward ethical leadership, learning how to respond appropriately to issues of not only right versus wrong, but issues of right versus right, understanding the possible benefits and consequences of their decisions. A wealth of examples is provided.

What is it about a career that moves our hearts and minds toward fulfilling a dream? It is our character. The truest approach to finding out who we are and what illuminates our lives is to look within. At the very heart of career development is good character. At the heart of good character is an individual who knows and loves the good, and seeks to share the good with others. By exploring careers and character together, we create internal and external environments that support and enhance each other, challenging students to lead conscious lives of personal quality and true richness every day.

Is there a difference between doing the right thing, and doing things right? Career questions ask, "What do you know about a specific career?" Character questions ask, "Now that you know about a specific career, what will you choose to do with what you know?" "How will you perform certain tasks and services for others, even when no one else is around?" "Will all individuals be given your best regardless of their socioeconomic background, physical condition, ethnicity, or religious beliefs?" Character questions often challenge the authenticity of what we say we believe and value in the workplace and in our personal lives.

Character and career questions together challenge us to pay attention to our lives and not fall asleep on the job. Career knowledge, self-knowledge, and ethical wisdom help us answer deeper questions about the meaning of work; they give us permission to transform our lives. Personal integrity is the price of admission.

The insight of one "ordinary" individual can make a difference in the world—if that one individual believes that character is an amazing gift to uncap knowledge and talents to empower the human community. Our world needs everyday heroes in the workplace—and "Careers with Character" challenges students to become those heroes.

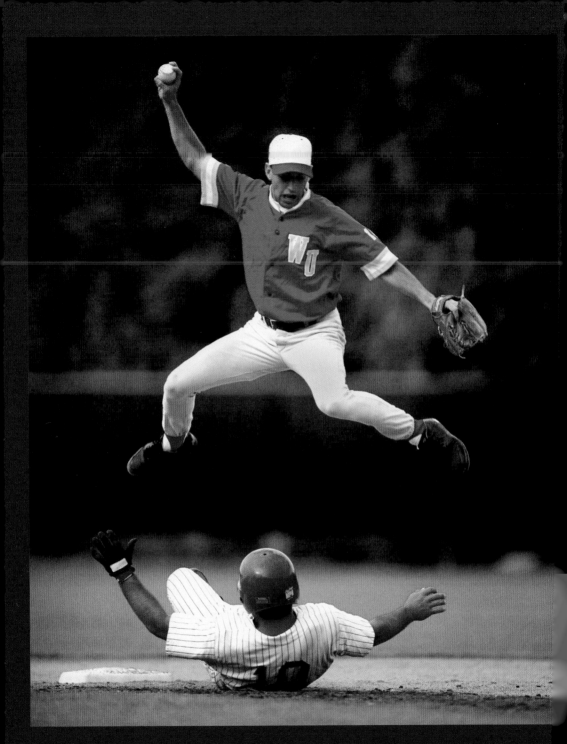

If you want to be a professional athlete, you need to find out what the job requires.

JOB REQUIREMENTS

Get ready now for the rest of your life!

CHAPTER ONE

I t's the bottom of the ninth inning, bases are loaded, and the count is three balls and two strikes. The next pitch will no doubt determine the outcome of the baseball game, which has the Philadelphia Phillies leading the Atlanta Braves by only one run. Atlanta is at bat, and there are two outs. The pitcher gets the signal from the catcher, and seconds later delivers a fast pitch. Usually when this pitcher throws his fastball, the batter never even sees it coming. But this time is different, and as the batter swings his bat, he connects; seconds later, the baseball is headed over the stadium wall. It's a grand slam, and the crowd goes wild! Atlanta scores, and the game is over!

Professional football players have plenty of excitement—but the competition for their jobs is stiff!

Scenes like this one inspire many young people to think about a career as a professional athlete or even a professional sports official. We are a nation of sports fans—and sports players. Interest in watching sports continues to grow, resulting in expanding leagues, completely new leagues, and more and larger venues in which to witness amateur and professional competitions. Recreational participation in sports is at an all-time high as the general population seeks the benefits of sport and exercise for their positive effects on overall health and well-being. Some of those who participate in amateur sports dream of becoming paid professional athletes, coaches, or sports officials, but very few beat the long odds and have the opportunity to make a living as professional athletes. Those who do, find that careers are short and jobs are insecure—so having an alternative plan for a career is essential. For many, that alternative is a job in the ranks of coaches in amateur athletics, people who teach and direct their sports in high schools, colleges and universities, and clubs.

ATHLETES

Athletes compete in organized, officiated sports events to entertain spectators. When playing a game, they are required to understand the strategies of their game while obeying the rules and regulations of the sport. These events include both team sports—such as baseball, basketball, football, hockey, and soccer—and individual sports—such as golf, tennis, and bowling. As the type of sport varies, so does the level of play, ranging from unpaid high school athletics to professional sports, in which the best from around the world compete before national television audiences.

In addition to competing in athletic events, professional athletes spend many hours practicing skills and teamwork under the guidance of a coach or sports instructor. Most athletes practice hard for hours every day. They also spend additional hours viewing films, critiquing their own performances and techniques, and scouting their opponent's tendencies and weaknesses. Some athletes may also be advised by strength trainers in an effort to gain muscle and stamina while preventing injury. Competition at all levels is extremely in-

The Principles of Good Character

1. Your character is defined by what you do, not by what you say or believe.
2. Every choice you make helps define the kind of person you are choosing to be.
3. Good character requires doing the right thing, even when it is costly or risky.
4. You don't have to take the worst behavior of others as a standard for yourself. You can choose to be better than that.
5. What you do matters, and one person can make an important difference.
6. The payoff for good character is that it makes you a better person and it makes the world a better place.

From www.goodcharacter.com

Coach John Wooden's Philosophies of Life

1. Strive for perfection.
2. Do the best you can. That is what counts.
3. You'll get better cooperation and results if you are sincerely interested in people, their families and their interests.
4. Learn as if you were going to live forever, and live as if you were going to die tomorrow.
5. Be interested in finding the best way, not in having your own way.
6. Mix idealism with realism and add hard work.
7. Prepare properly; you may be outscored but you will never lose.

Adapted from www.charactercounts.org.

tense and job security is always precarious. As a result, many athletes train year-round to maintain excellent form, technique, and peak physical condition; very little downtime from the sport exists at the professional level. Athletes also must conform to regimented diets during the height of their sports season to supplement any physical training program. Many athletes push their bodies to the limit, so career-ending injury is always a risk. Even minor injuries to an athlete may be sufficient opportunity for another athlete to play, excel, and become a permanent replacement.

COACHES

These professionals organize, instruct, and teach amateur and professional athletes in the fundamentals of individual and team sports. In individual sports, instructors rather than coaches may often fill this role. Both coaches and instructors train athletes for competition by holding practice sessions to perform drills and improve the athlete's skills and conditioning. Using their expertise in the sport, coaches instruct the athlete on proper form and technique; later they give the athlete advanced exercises to maximize the player's potential. Along with overseeing athletes as they refine their indi-

Referees need extensive knowledge of their game so they can make decisions quickly.

vidual skills, coaches also are responsible for managing the team during both practice sessions and competitions. They may also select, store, issue, and inventory equipment, materials, and supplies. During competitions, coaches select players for optimum team chemistry and success. In addition, coaches direct team strategy and may call specific plays to surprise or overpower the opponent. To choose the best plays, coaches evaluate or "scout" the opposing team prior to the competition, using the information to determine game strategies and practice specific plays.

As coaches, advocating good sportsmanship, promoting a competitive spirit, tutoring fairness, and teaching teamwork are all important responsibilities. Many coaches in high schools are primarily teachers of academic subjects and supplement their income by coaching part-time. College coaches consider their jobs to be a full-time discipline and may be away from home frequently as they

Coaches have the opportunity to encourage players.

travel to scout and recruit prospective players. Coaches sacrifice many hours of their free time throughout their careers, particularly full-time coaches at the professional level, whose seasons are much longer than those at the amateur level.

UMPIRES, REFEREES, AND OTHER SPORTS OFFICIALS

These professionals officiate competitive athletic and sporting events. They observe the play, detect infractions of rules, and impose penalties established by the sports' regulations. Umpires, referees, and sports officials anticipate plays and position themselves to best see the action, assess the situation, and determine any violations. Some sports officials, such as boxing referees, may work independently, while others such as umpires—the sports officials of baseball—work in groups. Regardless of the sport, the job is highly stressful because officials are often required to assess the play and make a decision in a matter of a split second; many times competitors, coaches, and spectators disagree strenuously.

Education and training requirements for athletes, coaches, and sports officials vary greatly by the level and type of sport. Regardless of the sport or occupation, jobs require immense overall knowledge of the game, usually acquired through years of experience at lower levels. Athletes usually begin competing in their sports while in elementary or middle school and continue through high school and often college. They play in amateur tournaments and on high school and college teams, where the best attract the attention of professional scouts. Most schools require that participating athletes maintain specific academic standards to remain eligible to play.

The Cost of Character

Sports officials are often called on to make decisions based on character values. Whenever a sports rule is violated, officials have two choices: look the other way and not make the call—or interpret the rule literally and make a call that may be unpopular. Character Counts president Michael Josephson clarifies this dilemma by saying:

My point is not to say that you should be a strict-blind-eyed-never-look-at-the-consequences rule enforcer. When you decide to interpret a rule, the reason ought to be because you think it's advancing the purposes of the rule and the game, not in order to advance the entertainment or to protect your job or to affect anybody else. There are two kinds of ethical problems. One we call a problem of discernment. You're not sure what the right thing to do is. Did a player do something intentionally or not? If you're not sure, you have to be more careful. The second kind of ethical issues we face are problems of willpower. It's very clear what we should do, but we may not want to pay the cost.

Coaches are the minds behind football strategies.

Becoming a professional athlete is the culmination of years of effort. Athletes who seek to compete professionally must have extraordinary talent, desire, and dedication to training.

For high school coach and sports instructor jobs, schools usually first look to hire existing teachers willing to take on the jobs part-time. If no one suitable is found, the schools hire someone from outside. Some entry-level positions for coaches or instructors only require experience derived as a participant in the sport or activity. Many coaches begin their careers as assistant coaches to gain the necessary knowledge and experience needed to become a head coach. Head coach jobs at larger schools that strive to compete at the highest levels of a sport require substantial experience as a head coach at another school or as an assistant coach. To reach the ranks of professional coaching, it usually takes years of coaching experience and a winning record in the lower ranks.

Public secondary school coaches and sports instructors at all levels usually must have a bachelor's degree and meet state requirements for licensure as a teacher. Licensure may not be required for coach and sports instructor jobs in private schools. Degree programs specifically related to coaching include exercise and sports science, physiology, kinesiology, nutrition and fitness, physical education, and sports medicine.

For sports instructors, certification is highly desirable for those interested in becoming a tennis, golf, karate, or any other kind of instructor. Often one must be at least 18 years old and CPR certified. There are many certifying organizations specific to the various sports and their training requirements vary depending on their standards. Participation in a clinic, camp, or school usually is required for certification. Part-time workers and those in smaller facilities are less likely to need formal education or training.

Each sport has specific requirements for umpires, referees, and other sports officials. These professionals often begin their careers by volunteering for intramural, community, and recreational league competitions. For high school and college refereeing, candidates must be certified by an officiating school and get through a probationary period for evaluation. Some larger college conferences often require officials to have certification and other qualifications, such as residence in or near the conference boundaries along with previous experience that typically includes several years officiating high school, community college, or other college conference games.

Standards are even more stringent for officials

According to the Citizenship Through Sports Alliance, a collaboration of major professional and amateur sports organizations, there is "a worrisome decline in sportsmanship and ethical conduct in sports, a deterioration that permeates sports competition from the youth leagues to the professional leagues."

In professional sports. For nonprofessional baseball umpire jobs, for example, a high school diploma or equivalent is usually sufficient, plus 20/20 vision and quick reflexes. To qualify for the professional ranks, however, prospective candidates must attend professional umpire training school. Currently, there are three schools whose curriculums have been approved by the Professional Baseball Umpires Corporation (PBUC) for training. Top graduates are then selected for further evaluation while officiating in a rookie *minor league*. Umpires usually need eight to ten years of experience in various minor leagues before being considered for *major league* jobs.

Athletes, coaches, and sports officials must relate well to others and possess good communication and leadership skills. Coaches also must be resourceful and flexible to successfully instruct and motivate individuals or groups of athletes. If you are interested in either of those occupations as a career, you will find them to be both challenging and rewarding. There are many avenues you can follow to help you explore if either of these careers is right for you.

If you do choose one of these careers, remember: professional officials and athletes display their characters, for good or bad, when they are working, because the public watches their every move. Things like integrity and trustworthiness, respect and compassion, justice and fairness, responsibility, courage, self-discipline and diligence, and citizenship are important qualities for people who choose this career field. In the following chapters you will learn all about those character traits and how they will relate to a job in professional sports.

Legendary UCLA basketball coach John Wooden said, "You cannot attain and maintain physical condition unless you are morally and mentally conditioned. I tell my players that our team condition depends on two factors—how hard they work on the floor during practice and how well they behave between practices." In other words, character development is an important element in preparing for a professional career in sports.

Michael Josephson, the president of the Character Counts Coalition, teaches that character is embodied by several core values; these values make an important difference in people's lives. In professional sports, choosing to be a person who embodies good character allows athletes and officials to demonstrate these qualities on the playing field. As others watch their actions, these professionals have the power to shape our society in positive ways.

In the chapters that follow, we will look at the following character traits in more detail:

- Integrity and trustworthiness
- Respect and compassion
- Justice and fairness
- Responsibility
- Courage
- Self-discipline and diligence
- Citizenship

"Controlling our attitudes is not easy," Josephson admits. "It takes character to harness powerful and instinctive feelings and redirect our thoughts toward positive attitudes, but those who do live happier lives in a happier world."

If you want to explore your career options in professional coaching or athletics, learn as much as you can about the requirements of the sport that interests you. Understand that it will take hard work, determination . . . and above all, the right character.

Ability may get you to the top, but it takes character to keep you there.

—Coach John Wooden

Because children often use baseball players as their models, players need to possess outstanding integrity and trustworthiness.

INTEGRITY AND TRUSTWORTHINESS

Integrity means you don't make promises lightly. . . .

CHAPTER TWO

In 1962 on a spring day in El Dorado, Arkansas, a Little League team was practicing. All the players on the team loved to play baseball, including nine-year-old Billy Bradley. But Billy nearly died from a freak accident that occurred that day when lightning struck a tree near a water fountain from which he was drinking. The heat from the lightning bolt was so hot and intense that it even melted Billy's baseball cap.

Billy wasn't the only one injured from the lightning strike. Several other players and coaches were also knocked to the ground; when they were able to stand up again they discovered that Billy was unconscious. He was barely breathing, and one of the coaches

Baseball players don't just play the game; they also can use their role to help others.

began CPR. Thankfully, by the time the ambulance arrived, Billy was once again breathing normally, but for the next several days he remained unconscious.

When Billy finally woke up, the doctors realized he had lost his sight. They were not sure if his loss was temporary, or if the damage to his eyesight might be permanent. A few hours later the doctors discovered that the heat from the lightning had burned his eyes. Doctors were hopeful that a famous eye surgeon by the name of Dr. Louis Girard would be able to restore Billy's sight, and they soon found out that he would require six painful operations, three on each eye. His family would have to take him to Houston to the Methodist Hospital for the surgery.

During that same year the Colt 45s (now known as the Houston Astros) joined the National League and started playing in Houston, Texas. Young boys from the Arkansas area quickly started considering the Colt 45s their hometown team, since it was the closest major league club to their state. As Billy was recuperating from his injuries, he would listen to the Colt 45s baseball games on the radio in

A baseball player who values integrity will keep his promises—both on and off the playing field.

his hospital room. Billy's favorite baseball player on that team was third baseman Bob Aspromonte.

News of Billy's accident reached the Colt 45 team and when Aspromonte heard that the youngster was in Houston for an operation, he and several other ballplayers visited Billy in the hospital. They brought team souvenirs and a brand new radio so he could listen to the ball games from his hospital room.

People who value integrity and trustworthiness:

- tell the truth.
- don't withhold important information.
- are sincere; they don't deceive, mislead, try to trick others.
- don't betray a trust.
- don't steal.
- don't cheat.
- stand up for beliefs about right and wrong.
- keep their promises.

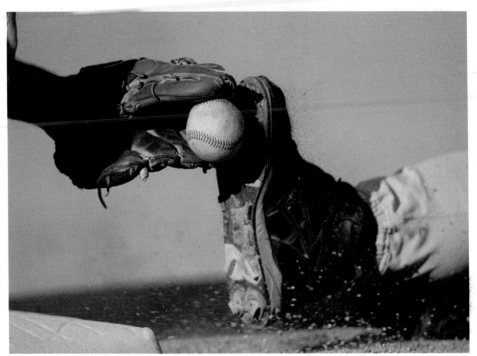

Baseball is full of moments when the game could go either way.

On the night before Billy's first operation, his parents took him to a home game for the Colt 45s. Although Billy couldn't see the game, he could listen, and he was allowed to visit Aspromonte in the Houston locker room. The baseball player was able to calm some of the boy's fears about the operation. He told Billy he had to believe he would see again; before Billy knew it, Aspromonte assured him, he would find himself enjoying a Little League game with his friends. When Aspromonte asked Billy if he could do anything for him, Billy responded by asking him to hit a home run in his honor.

Aspromonte could have simply told the boy what he wanted to hear. But the ballplayer knew he might not be able to keep his promise. He told Billy he was more of a base-hit batter than a home-run batter, and asked if Billy would accept a base hit instead. When Aspromonte saw how disappointed Billy looked, he vowed to try as

Baseball players inspire us all with their heroic integrity.

The Rest of the Story

Bob Aspromonte retired from baseball in 1971. Three years later, he was working on a car when the battery exploded in his face. The doctors told him that the battery acid had blinded him, and that in order to restore his eyesight he would need to go to that same hospital in Houston where Billy had gone. The same doctor, Dr. Louis Girard, would be the one performing the eye surgery.

Billy heard about the accident and telephoned his friend; he told him to have faith that his vision would soon be restored. Billy reminded Aspromonte that he had helped Billy through a similar ordeal. Thanks to the surgery, Aspromonte was able to have over 50 percent of his eyesight restored.

Sometimes, the people to whom we show integrity and trustworthiness have a chance to return the favor.

hard as he could to hit a home run in Billy's honor. He didn't want to lie; he didn't want to promise something he couldn't deliver. But he could tell Billy he would do the best he could; he committed himself to being worthy of the boy's trust.

The first three times Aspromonte was at bat he didn't even get a base hit. Billy had to return to the hospital before the game was over, disappointed because he didn't think his friend would be able to hit that home run in his honor. He listened to the last few innings of the game on his new portable radio in his hospital room. In the bottom of the eighth inning, the Houston team was losing to the San Francisco Giants by a score of three to one. When Aspromonte took his turn at bat, he missed the first pitch, and Billy was afraid his hero was going to strike out. More determined than ever, however, Aspromonte swung at that second pitch—and the ball soared high and deep toward the left field fence. It was a home run!

Children playing games on the playground often imitate real-life sports figures.

Billy was elated when he heard the excitement of the crowd on the radio. His hero had come through for him. After the game, Aspromonte was interviewed by a *sportscaster* from a radio station, and the ballplayer told everyone that the home run he had hit was for Billy, who was in the hospital. The next day the headlines of the local paper told about the ballplayer who had promised to hit a home run for a youngster who needed eye surgery.

After the first operation, Billy was able to see light and shadows. His eyesight was on the way to being returned to normal, but he still had a few more operations to go. The following year, Billy was once again at that hospital in Houston, waiting for another eye operation. The surgery was a success, and Billy's eyesight was almost back to normal. His parents took him to see the Colts play a home game in Houston, and Billy asked Aspromonte if he could hit another home run for him. This time Billy would be able to see it with his own eyes.

Aspromonte did not make this promise any more easily than he had the earlier one. The ballplayer told Billy he would try his best, but he wasn't sure if he could pull off a home run; they would be playing the Chicago Cubs, a tough team. Aspromonte could only say he would try his hardest—and once again, he was able to hit a home run. The crowd went wild, and so did Billy.

Six weeks later, Billy had his final eye surgery in Houston, and Aspromonte was faced with yet another request for a home run. This time he was able to hit a grand slam, his second of the season; he helped the Colts beat the New York Mets seven to three. Everyone was happy, especially Billy, who was finally able to return home and begin playing Little League baseball once again. His goal was to be like Bob Aspromonte, and Billy practiced and worked hard; three years after being struck by lightning, he pitched his first *no-hitter* baseball game.

Bob Aspromonte made a difference in Billy's life. The ballplayer didn't give his word easily, simply to say what was expected of him. Instead, he was careful to promise only what he could realistically deliver. He committed himself to doing the best for a young boy who needed hope—and as a result, Billy Bradley knew he could trust Aspromonte. The ballplayer's integrity gave Billy courage and inspiration for his entire life.

If you choose a career in sports, whether as an athlete or as a coach or other sports official, you too will have many opportunities to touch the lives of young people. If you are committed to a life of integrity, you will earn their trust—and like Bob Aspromonte, you will inspire them to be all they can be.

You have to expect things of yourself before you can do them.
—Michael Jordan, basketball star

Football players rely on the respect and compassion of their coaches.

RESPECT AND COMPASSION

Can you show others respect . . . even when they aren't respecting you?

CHAPTER THREE

I n 1971, the Alexandria City Council voted to integrate T. C. Williams High School, a decision that was criticized by many in the community. The Vietnam War was still dragging along, and on the domestic front, relations between people of different races were strained and unstable. T. C. Williams High was one of the first schools to be *integrated* in the State of Virginia.

During the summer of 1971, Coach Herman Boone, an African American who had been coaching in North Carolina, secured the head coach position at T.C. Williams High School, a move that infuriated the white football players and coaching staff already in place at the school. Many of the football players threatened to leave the

Coach Boone demonstrated his respect for each member of his team, regardless of race.

team and not play football at all, rather than play for an African American coach. Mr. Bill Yoast had been the assistant coach at T.C. Williams High School and was next in line to be named head coach. . . and then Coach Boone arrived on the scene. Coach Yoast remained the assistant coach of the football team, but he was so upset that he considered retiring from coaching football. After a rocky beginning, however, Coach Boone and Coach Yoast focused on the same goal: to have the best football team in Virginia, and the country, a goal that they achieved. The T.C. Williams Titans won every game they played, and ended the season as the second-best high school team in the nation.

The trials and tribulations of those events at T. C. Williams High School were captured on film in the Disney movie *Remember the Titans*. In the movie, Denzel Washington played the part of coach Herman Boone, and the entire world was able to see how that professional athletic coach used respect and compassion to get his players to work together toward a common goal.

When he was first offered the job as head coach, Coach Boone didn't think he deserved the job. He felt that Bill Yoast had paid his dues and had earned the right to take over the top position. In an interview with the web site *Blackathlete.com*, Boone talked about how difficult his job was at first. He knew no one in his new community respected him; they thought he was inferior simply because he was an African American. But despite the prejudice he faced, he unfailingly demonstrated compassion and respect for the students with whom he worked. "It's about communication," he said in the interview, "talking to each other. We forced the kids to spend time with each other, to find things out about each other, and that was very helpful."

By showing respect and compassion to all of the players and other coaches, Boone proved he cared about the rights and feelings of others. He wanted to show everyone, including the parents and everyone else in the town, that treating others the way you want to be treated is a key ingredient in becoming a

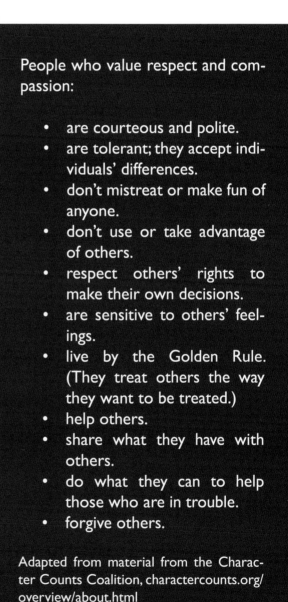

People who value respect and compassion:

- are courteous and polite.
- are tolerant; they accept individuals' differences.
- don't mistreat or make fun of anyone.
- don't use or take advantage of others.
- respect others' rights to make their own decisions.
- are sensitive to others' feelings.
- live by the Golden Rule. (They treat others the way they want to be treated.)
- help others.
- share what they have with others.
- do what they can to help those who are in trouble.
- forgive others.

Adapted from material from the Character Counts Coalition, charactercounts.org/overview/about.html successful athlete or coach. Boone realized that when a player has good self-esteem, he is also able to respect both himself and others. Boone did what he could to build that esteem in his players.

One scene in the movie was based on a real-life incident involving two students: Gerry Bertier, who is white, and Julius Campbell, who is black. Both were extraordinary football players who started out as bitter enemies, but they overcame the odds and became best friends. At first the two students wanted nothing to do with each other. But Coach Boone knew he had to show the players they couldn't work together without respect—and in order for them to respect one another, he was going to have to get them to understand each other, and finally to like each other.

As the players arrived at training camp, Coach Boone told Gerry and Julius they had to share a room. At first they didn't speak to

A football team should have enough respect for each other that they can play together as a single unit.

Respect for others is important, but so is respect for yourself; sports build self-respect.

The National Federation of State High School Associations is the national service and administrative organization of high school athletics. Its members believe that respect is very important for all athletes. This is how its charter defines respect:

Holding oneself and others in high regard. Through emphasis on sportsmanship (which has at its heart respect for self and others), athletes can learn valuable lessons about respect even during the heat of competition. These lessons can extend beyond the playing field to a healthy respect for others' talents and abilities, and a high regard for one's own integrity. Coaches can help athletes apply these concepts to their lives outside of sports.

Coach Boone used the qualities of good character to create a united and powerful team.

When a coach demonstrates his respect and compassion for a discouraged player, he improves the entire team.

each other; eventually, they got into a fight. But Coach Boone didn't give up. He forced the two students, as well as the rest of the players on the team, to get to know each other. He realized that once the students found out how much they had in common they would stop seeing each other as the enemy. Then they could start working together toward their common goal: creating a winning football team.

Over the next few days the students continued to grumble—but eventually they learned to respect one another. Coach Boone could see the changes in many of the players, and by the end of the training camp everyone had started playing together as a single unit—a unit that was bound and determined to work as hard as they possibly could to have a winning football season.

Coach Herman Boone met the challenge and helped bring the team to victory. Along the way he may have used steps like these to help him act with respect and compassion:

1. *He recognized that he was faced with a moral issue.* In this case, it was the racial dividing lines. Sometimes when we see a problem, it is much easier to ignore it and hope that it goes away or solves itself. But problems must be dealt with, and Coach Boone knew he had to instill a sense of respect and compassion among the players in order to get them working as one team.

2. *He made a decision to move forward.* Coach Boone had some difficult decisions to make, and he made them after carefully studying the problems. He didn't allow himself to freeze; he didn't take so long to decide on a course of action that it was too late to do anything.

3. *He monitored and modified his decisions.* After Coach Boone saw that some progress was being made among the players, it was easier for him to come up with new solutions to keep everyone moving forward. He kept track of what was happening, and he remained committed to his goals.

One day, you too may be a coach who faces a tough challenge like Coach Boone encountered. In the meantime, how can you apply these three steps to the challenges you meet in your life today?

You cannot attain and maintain physical condition unless you are morally and mentally conditioned. . . . I always told my players that our team condition depended on two factors—how hard they worked on the floor during practice and how well they behaved between practices.

—Coach John Wooden

In 2002, the judges of the pair-skating competition at the Winter Olympics faced a dilemma that concerned justice and fairness.

JUSTICE AND FAIRNESS

When individuals are treated unfairly, the entire world is damaged in some way.

CHAPTER FOUR

On February 12, 2002, in Salt Lake City, Utah, the Winter Olympics were in full swing. Record numbers of viewers were watching the events on television, and the crowds in the local venues were filled to capacity. Everyone was happy and proud to be part of Olympic history in the making.

As the Monday night Olympic figure skating pairs competition was winding down to a close, the crowd was sure the gold medal would go to Jamie Sale and David Pelletier of Canada. When the judges instead awarded the first-place gold medal to the Russian skaters, Yelena Berezhnaya and Anton Sikharulidze, the crowd booed the judges' decision. Just about everyone who was there had

The Russians had been champions in the pair-skating competition since 1964.

felt certain the Canadians' free-skating performance was nearly perfect. While they agreed that the Russian skaters were good, their performance couldn't compare to the Canadians'.

Jamie Sale and David Pelletier were very disappointed by the judges' decision. Sale was caught on camera crying, and Pelletier hid his face in his hands. They had thought for sure that they were going to win the gold medal that evening at the Winter Olympics. The next morning on the NBC *Today Show*, David Pelletier told everyone, "It was like somebody punched me in the stomach."

The Russians had won the pairs-skating gold medals for ten straight championships since 1964, and the pressure for this year's Olympic event was enormous. But so many people had witnessed a near-perfect performance from the Canadian couple and a somewhat flawed performance by the Russian couple that cries of foul and unfair ran rampant. Canada's Olympic delegation was insulted by the results, and they called for an immediate investigation into the decision that gave the Russians the gold medal over the Canadians. "I was horrified," said Sally Rehorick, Canadian Delegation Chief and 25-year figure skating judge. "When Jamie and David fin-

Judges need to use all the justice and fairness they possess when judging an Olympic event.

People who value justice and fairness:

- treat all people the same (as much as possible).
- are open-minded; they are willing to listen to others' points of views and try to understand.
- consider carefully before making decisions that affect others.
- don't take advantage of others' mistakes.
- don't take more than their fair share.
- cooperate with others.
- recognize the uniqueness and value of each individual.

Adapted from material from the Character Counts Coalition, character-counts.org/overview/about.html

ished skating, I said, 'Oh, that's easy.' Anton made a major error on his double axel, Elena had a stiff knee on her second landing and they didn't come down as easily. The unison was achieved with Jamie and David in a much more intricate way."

The 1984 Olympic Champion, Scott Hamilton, agreed with Rehorick and said, "The Canadians won that program. There's not a doubt from anyone in the place except maybe a few judges."

A few days later, after an investigation had been launched, one of the judges admitted she had yielded to pressure from a member of the French federation. The International Skating Union charged her with *misconduct* and recommended the International Olympic Committee consider the Canadians as cochampions. The Olympic Committee decided to award gold medals to both the Russians and the Canadians in the figure skating pairs event because of the misconduct on the part of at least one of the judges.

Jacque Rogge, attending his first Olympic Games as the IOC President, said, "It's happened in the past, and we hope it's not going to happen in the future. But we took a decision that was out of justice and fairness for the athletes." Canadian pair Jamie Sale and David Pelletier said they were "truly honored" at finally receiving figure skating gold medals.

Athletes who compete in any type of competition, whether it's at the high school level, college level, professional level, or the Olympics, have a right to expect justice and fair treatment from officials and judges who are charged with officiating those events. When sports officials yield to pressures to influence their decisions, these officials devalue the athletes' genuine efforts. For both the spectators and the participants, the competition becomes meaningless. That's why justice and fairness are such important character values for these professionals. Professional and amateur sports athletes, of-

The Winter Olympics of 2002 was the eighth time in Olympic history that medals were changed or awarded after the competition had taken place. The last time a duplicate gold was awarded, in the 1992 Olympic Games, it also went to a Canadian. Synchronized swimmer Sylvie Frechette was upgraded from silver after a scoring error was discovered on the judges' scorecards.

In the 1992 Olympic Games, an error was discovered on the scorecards. Human error can't always be avoided—but intentional injustice can be.

Excuses We Make for Unethical Behavior

- *If it's "necessary" then it's the right thing to do.* The ends do not justify the means.
- *If it's legal, it's okay.* The law sets only a minimal standard of behavior; being unkind, telling a lie to a friend, or taking more than your share of dessert are not crimes—but they are still unethical.
- *I was just doing it for you.* Sometimes we tell "white lies" or evade the truth to avoid hurting another's feelings—when in fact, although the truth may be uncomfortable, it will do the other person good to hear it.
- *I'm just fighting fire with fire; everybody does it.* The behavior of those around you does not excuse your lack of fairness or other unethical behaviors. There is no safety in numbers!
- *It doesn't hurt anyone.* We often underestimate the cost of failing to do the right thing.
- *It's okay so long as I don't gain personally.* Although our actions may help some individuals, however, other individuals—including ourselves—are sure to suffer as a consequence of our unethical behavior.
- *I've got it coming; I deserve to take more than my share because I worked more than anyone else.* The Golden Rule applies here: would you want others to behave the same way?

Adapted from materials from the Josephson Institute of Ethics, josephsoninstitute.org

ficials, and judges all must be of high moral character and display the character traits of a person who knows the importance of always doing the right thing.

What roles do justice and fairness play in your life?

Injustice anywhere is a threat to justice everywhere.
—Martin Luther King, Jr.

College football coaches have many responsibilities—and living their lives with character is one of the most important.

RESPONSIBILITY

*A sense of responsibility inspires us to live a
life of character . . . year after year.*

CHAPTER FIVE

Harold Raymond was born on November 14, 1926, in Flint,
Michigan, and was given the nickname "Tubby" by his child-
hood playmates. Even though he eventually lost the weight,
the nickname stuck with him the rest of his life. He went on to graduate from the University of Michigan with a degree in education, and
then he received a master's degree in human development from the
University of Delaware. He fell in love with Delaware, and he began
his career there as a football coach in 1966.

For three decades, Tubby coached the Delaware Blue Hens;
then, on February 18, 2002, he announced that he was retiring.
Players had always respected him and considered him to be a responsible coach. Not too many professional coaches last that long
in one position, but Tubby was different. He really loved his work.

Being responsible means you do your best.

Over the years he has won many awards, including the Maxwell Football Club's Tri-State Coach of the Year. (The award honors a local high school or college coach who inspires his players to succeed at the next level, be that football or the business world.) Some people burn out after enough years in the same profession. But not Tubby. He has always insisted that every year was different; the only things that remained the same were the football and the one hundred yards you play it on. He was inducted into the State of Delaware Sports Hall of Fame in 1993, and received the Vince Lombardi Football

Being responsible means:

- to make sure your behavior shows you can be trusted.
- to make sure you consider the feelings of others.
- to take responsibility for your own actions and accept the consequences.
- to do your best, no matter what the circumstances.
- to not make excuses for what has happened.

Responsible coaches may not always lead their teams to victory—but they do make sure their teams play the best they possibly can.

The Canadian Professional Coaches Association has adopted a Coaching Code of Ethics. Under the section titled "Responsible Coaching," it reads in part:

The principle of responsible coaching carries the basic ethical expectation that the activities of coaches will benefit society in general and participants in particular and will do no harm. Fundamental to the implementation of this principle is the notion of competence—responsible coaching (maximizing benefits and minimizing risks to participants) is performed by coaches who are "well prepared and current" in their discipline.

In addition, responsible coaching means that coaches

1. act in the best interest of the athlete's development as a whole person;
2. recognize the power inherent in the position of coach;
3. are aware of their personal values and how these affect their practice as coaches;
4. acknowledge the limitations of their discipline; and
5. accept the responsibility to work with other coaches and professionals in sport.

Foundation Lifetime Achievement Award in 1999. In 2000, he was recognized by *Sports Illustrated* as one of the top 100 sports figures of the 20th century in the State of Delaware. In 2003, he received one of the greatest honors of all—Tubby was inducted into the College Football Hall of Fame.

On November 10, 2001, Tubby marked his 300th win and became the ninth coach in college football history to win so many games. He is the fourth coach in history to win all 300 games at the same school, joining such famous names as Eddie Robinson, Joe Paterno, and Roy Kidd.

Words of Wisdom from Two Great Coaches

Don't let what you cannot do interfere with what you can do.

The athlete who says that something cannot be done should never interrupt the one who is doing it.

—John Wooden, UCLA coach

Great football coaches have the vision to see, the faith to believe, the courage to do ... and 25 great players.

Styles of coaching may differ—from bombastic to philosophical. But at the end of the day, any good coach is a teacher.

—Mark Levy, football coach

Great football coaches see the game from both a close-up view—and from a larger perspective.

No matter what teams were playing, Coach Tubby Raymond felt a personal sense of responsibility to every player and coach in the stadium; he made sure that everyone was treated well, both on and off the field. He earned the admiration of many other college football coaches, including Villanova coach Andy Talley. When Talley learned of Tubby's retirement, he told reporters, "He's a legend and I'm going to miss our competition. He was very special, one of the greatest coaches of all time."

Tubby got his 300th victory at the expense of Richmond coach Jim Reid, who said, "The coaching profession is a lot poorer today because Tubby is retiring. I can't tell you how much I respect him, as a coach and as a man. He won a lot of games, and even more importantly, he turned out a lot of solid citizens. Kids who played for him learned about life as well as football."

Coach Tubby Raymond loved his job as a coach, but he also loved his job as a role model for students. He recognized that his responsibilities were greater than merely leading his team to victory. As a leader of character, he was responsible not only to his team but to the entire human community. He may have retired from coaching the Delaware Blue Hens, but he will always be remembered as a man with great character.

How do you think you will be remembered?

Success is peace of mind, which is a direct result of self satisfaction in knowing you did your best to become the best that you are capable of becoming.

—John Wooden

The great baseball players of history continue to inspire us today with their courage.

COURAGE

Courage means speaking up for what you believe . . . and sometimes it means keeping quiet.

CHAPTER SIX

On July 4, 1939, when Yankee slugger Lou Gehrig took the field to announce that after 19 years in baseball he was retiring, he was met by a roaring crowd. Everyone who enjoyed baseball loved this shy, quiet man. Even people who didn't follow the game knew the story of the player fondly referred to as the "Iron Horse."

This was a man who could be depended upon to maintain his cool in the heat of the game and deliver a hit. This was the athlete who, in 1932, accomplished what no other baseball player ever had—he hit four home runs in four consecutive times at bat. Fans

Baseball is full of moments of heroism.

Being responsible means:

- to make sure your behavior shows you can be trusted.
- to make sure you consider the feelings of others.
- to take responsibility for your own actions and accept the consequences.
- to do your best, no matter what the circumstances.
- to not make excuses for what has happened.

marveled at everything about the heroic player, both professionally and personally; he had never missed playing a game since beginning his career in 1925, and after becoming successful, he had generously given his parents a new home.

Lou spoke into the microphone to thank the fans in Yankee Stadium and tell them, "Today I think I'm the luckiest man alive. . . . I may have been given a bad break, but I have an awful lot to live for."

Lou Gehrig had a debilitating and fatal disease that has since been named after him. Everyone admired the courage the "Iron Horse" displayed on the field and off—for Lou Gehrig didn't retire from life when he retired from baseball. As he walked off the field, Mayor LaGuardia asked Lou if he would become a member of the New York City parole board, and Lou agreed.

Often people's acts of courage are recognized immediately, but sometimes this is not the case. Courageous acts can go unrecognized, and people may even scorn heroes for many years because of their actions. When the now-beloved boxer Muhammad Ali objected to the draft because of his religious and moral principles and refused to enter the service, he was forced to relinquish his championship title and was even put in jail. Today most people think the Vietnam War was a mistake for the United States, and we admire Muhammad Ali because he stood up for his beliefs.

Some situations require courageous action; other times people demonstrate their courage by displaying fortitude and resolve. This was the case with Jackie Robinson when he "broke the color barrier" in baseball in the late 1940s.

In those days African Americans who wanted to play professional baseball were forced to play in the Negro League. As early as the 1930s, however, sports writers in several newspapers began calling for the integration of baseball.

Branch Rickey was involved with baseball in a variety of capacities—as a player, coach, manager, and owner—for more than 60 years. His Hall of Fame plaque mentions both his creation of baseball's farm system in the 1920s and his signing of Jackie Robinson. Rickey's interest in integrating baseball began early in his career. He had been particularly troubled by the policy of barring African Americans from grandstand seating in St. Louis, when he worked for the Cardinals.

Dodgers' Charles Johnson stretches in front of a mural of Jackie Robinson. Today, baseball players are judged by their skills rather than the color of their skin.

The *Pittsburgh Courier's* Wendell Smith and the *Daily Worker's* Lester Rodney were especially vocal and influential in this campaign.

When the United States entered World War II, it took baseball players away from the game. Meanwhile, it also became increasingly difficult to deny equality when so many African Americans were demonstrating their courage on the battlefield. The time was more than

In 1945, when Rickey approached Jackie Robinson, baseball was being proposed as one of the first areas of American society to integrate. Not until 1948 did a presidential order desegregate the armed forces; the Supreme Court forbid *segregated* public schools in 1954.

ripe for change when Branch Rickey, the general manager of the Brooklyn Dodgers, took action.

Branch Rickey had been longing for the integration of baseball for some time. He knew that the Dodgers needed more than a great player; they needed someone who would be able to stand up to tremendous pressure, criticism, and unfair treatment. They needed someone who would be a silent hero, someone whose actions would be exemplary and would speak louder than words.

Born in 1919, Jackie Robinson was an all-around athlete excelling at every sport he tried, including football, basketball, track, tennis, and swimming as well as baseball. He was awarded varsity letters in four sports while attending the University of California, Los Angeles (UCLA) and had served in the Army before joining the Kansas City Monarchs, a team in the Negro Baseball League. As an athlete, Jackie Robinson was used to facing his adversaries head on.

When Branch Rickey met with him to discuss integration of the major leagues, Rickey explained that he was looking for someone with a different kind of courage. Rickey discussed some of the situations that could arise if Robinson joined the Dodgers. They even acted out several scenarios to be certain Jackie understood exactly what would be expected of him. In 1945, Jackie Robinson signed with the Dodgers and began playing for their minor league *farm* team, the Montreal Royals, in Canada. After a year of successful play in Canada, Jackie was transferred to the major league team in Brooklyn, New York, where he began to receive hate mail, just as

Do you have Jackie Robinson's courage?

If someone heckled you on the playing field or elsewhere would you:
- tell them to shut up?
- confront them by explaining why their comment didn't make sense?
- ignore them and walk away?

Rickey had expected. Robinson even received letters threatening his family, but he faced these private challenges just as bravely as he faced the public hecklers at the Dodgers games. His quiet dignity gained the respect and admiration of the nation. Other African American players were quickly signed as Jackie Robinson paved the way for them.

Some Facts About Jackie Robinson

- When Jackie Robinson was playing for the Dodgers, the team won six pennants: 1947, 1949, 1952, 1953, 1955, and 1956.
- In 1949, Jackie had his best season in baseball. He had the highest batting average in the National League, and the most stolen bases.
- In 1955, the Dodgers played against the Yankees in the World Series and won.
- Jackie Robinson considered winning the World Series one of the greatest thrills of his life.

He who is not courageous enough to take risks will accomplish nothing in life.

—Muhammad Ali, boxing champion

To be successful in any sport, you will need plenty of self-discipline and diligence.

SELF-DISCIPLINE AND DILIGENCE

If we are self-disciplined and diligent, we will accept hardships and frustrations—and never give up.

CHAPTER SEVEN

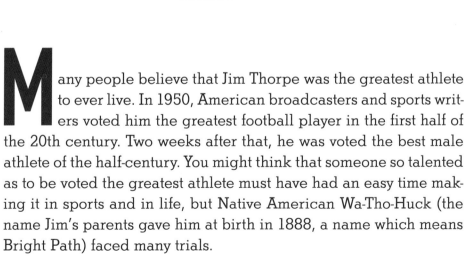

Many people believe that Jim Thorpe was the greatest athlete to ever live. In 1950, American broadcasters and sports writers voted him the greatest football player in the first half of the 20th century. Two weeks after that, he was voted the best male athlete of the half-century. You might think that someone so talented as to be voted the greatest athlete must have had an easy time making it in sports and in life, but Native American Wa-Tho-Huck (the name Jim's parents gave him at birth in 1888, a name which means Bright Path) faced many trials.

At the age of 16, Jim enrolled in the Carlisle Indian School in Pennsylvania. One day in 1907, Jim noticed the track team practicing the high jump. The bar was at five feet and nine inches, and no

Self-discipline and diligence pay off!

one could clear it. Jim thought that he would be able to jump that high and asked if he could give it a try. The team members thought it would be amusing to watch Jim, dressed in his work overalls, attempt the jump, so they agreed. On his first attempt, he cleared the bar! The track coach invited Jim to join the track team, and Jim went on to break all of the school's track and field records that year. By the next year he was breaking national records.

But Jim dreamed of playing football with the varsity team. He was not allowed to try out for that team, because he was too small. Eventually, though, he grew tall enough and gain enough weight to make the varsity team.

Most summers Jim did farm labor for money, but one summer he had the opportunity to play baseball for $15 to $25 per week. This was a violation of the athletic rules for amateur sports, although it was rather common for college students to do this, using false names. Jim Thorpe, however, used his own name. Back at college, his reputation continued to grow.

Soon Jim was training for the track and field events of the 1912 Olympics to be held in Stockholm, Sweden. Jim kept up his train-

Self-disciplined players keep going even when the going gets rough. Jim Thorpe represents a tremendous example of self-discipline.

ing by running on deck as his ship crossed the ocean. Jim won gold medals for both the Pentathlon and Decathlon and told reporters that when the King of Sweden shook his

People who value self-discipline and diligence:

- work to control their emotions, words, actions, and impulses
- give their best in all situations
- keep going even when the going is rough
- are determined and patient
- try again even when they fail the first time
- look for ways to do their work better

Adapted from material from the Character Education Network

Practice is an important part of any sports player's work.

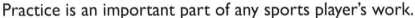

hand and awarded him his Olympic medals, it was the proudest moment of his life. The United States Commissioner of the Olympic games, James E. Sullivan, said that Jim was, "unquestionably the greatest athlete who ever lived." The U.S. Olympic team received a ticker-tape parade in New York City when they arrived back home.

Jim then returned to Carlisle for one more year. While at Carlisle, Jim didn't just compete in football and track. He also enjoyed lacrosse, tennis, handball, golf, swimming, bowling, gymnastics, rowing, figure skating, hockey, billiards, and he was captain of the basketball team! Before the football season was even over, several major league baseball representatives were bidding for him.

Then disaster struck. A reporter revealed that Jim had spent time playing baseball for money, and Jim's Olympic medals were stripped away! If you were paid to play a sport, you were considered to be a professional athlete (no matter how little money you had

Words of Wisdom from Sports Stars Who Were Diligent

Never give up and sit and grieve. Find another way.
—Satchel Paige, baseball star

I try to do the right thing at the right time. They may just be little things, but usually they make the difference between winning and losing.
—Kareem Abdul Jabbar, basketball star

I've lost the title two times, but I knew the only thing that would stop me was if I quit on myself. You have to face your challenges and give your all.
—Evander Holyfield, boxing champion

The greatest inventions in the world had hundreds of failures before the answers were found.
—Michael Jordan, basketball star

Nothing is going to be handed to you. You have to make things happen.
—Florence Griffith Joyner, Olympic track star

Most of us who aspire to be tops in our fields don't really consider the amount of work required to stay tops.
—Althea Gibson, tennis champion

received), and at this time, professional athletes were not allowed to compete in the Olympics. Jim wrote to the secretary of the Amateur Athletic Union (AAU) to explain that he hadn't really played for the money but rather simply for the love of the game. He thought everyone had known that he played since he had used his real name, and baseball scouts for the major leagues had seen him play. He didn't know he had done anything wrong. Nevertheless, the AAU voted to strip Jim Thorpe of his records and remove his name from athletic annuals. Many people stood up for Jim and wrote letters on his behalf, but his Olympic medals were returned to Sweden. F.R. Bie, from Norway was then declared to have won the Pentathlon, but he replied that Thorpe had won it. H. Wieslander of Sweden was declared to have won the Decathlon, but he said that he did not win and that the greatest athlete in the world was still Jim Thorpe.

Some people said that having to give back his Olympic medals broke Jim Thorpe's heart, but the story doesn't end here. The grandson of Chief Black Hawk of the Fox and Sac people was still wanted by baseball. St. Louis, Chicago, Pittsburgh, and Cincinnati all made offers, but Jim Thorpe decided to play for the New York Giants (though he later played for Cincinnati and Boston as well). Jim didn't just play baseball, though. Each autumn when baseball season ended, he played football for the Ohio Bulldogs, and he led them to a World Championship in 1916. In 1920, he assisted in the formation of the American Professional Football Association and became its first president. In 1922, hoping to open a door for more Native Americans to play football, he established an all-Indian team, but the team only lasted for two years. Jim Thorpe finally retired from baseball in 1928 and from football in 1929.

Throughout his life Jim cared about the problems of Native American people. He gave speeches in schools without payment even though it was sometimes difficult for him to cover his own travel expenses. Jim Thorpe was active on behalf of youth in sports until he died in 1953. Thirty years later, the International Olympic Committee made duplicate Olympic medals, which they presented to Jim Thorpe's children, and returned his name to the lists of Olympic champions.

Although Jim Thorpe could have given up on sports early in his life, he had the determination to keep trying. He would never have been as successful without self-discipline and diligence.

These are important character traits for anyone planning a career in professional sports. When you encounter failure, you can't give up, not if you hope to eventually achieve victory. Self-discipline and diligence are powerful character traits that inspire people to give their best, time after time, despite frustration and difficulty. These characteristics are not showy or spectacular—but they have helped many professional sports figures become successful on and off the field.

What about you? Have you developed the character traits necessary to be victorious?

Most of the important things in the world have been accomplished by people who have kept on trying when there seemed no hope at all.

—Herbert Meyer

Many sports players give back to their community by contributing to Little League teams.

CITIZENSHIP

*Citizenship means we give back some of
what we have been given.*

CHAPTER EIGHT

When it comes to good citizenship, professional athletes have really stepped up to the plate. Well-known teams and individual players are in a unique position to use their fame and reputation to set a positive example within their communities by doing good works and by raising funds for charitable organizations. Both in the United States and in Canada, sports teams hold annual athletic competitions and other fundraisers for countless good causes. Some of the most notable athletes have established their own foundations for charitable giving.

Here are some other examples of athletes who have used their fame and good fortune to give something back to the human community:

- Curtis Joseph (often referred to as CuJo), a retired Canadian hockey goalie who last played for the Toronto Maple Leafs, is another athlete who gives back to his community. CuJo's Kids allows sick children to enjoy hockey games because they can view the game comfortably by sitting in Curtis Joseph's special suite. CuJo's Crease is a room at the local hospital that has been outfitted with state-of-the-art anesthetic equipment for the treatment of children. What really makes it special for kids is that the room has been decorated to look like the Maple Leafs' dressing room.

- Albert Pujols, an MLB player with the Los Angeles Angels, is known for his charity work. He runs the Pujols Family Foundation, which assists children with Down's Syndrome in the United States, as well as underprivileged people in the Dominican Republic. He received the Roberto Clemente award in 2008, given to players who give back to their communities in significant ways.

- Retired professional Canadian figure skater Elvis Stojko has established scholarships for children with financial need who are interested in figure skating. He was also the children's ambassador for the Ronald McDonald Foundation.

- Vince Carter of the Dallas Mavericks basketball team has established Vince's Embassy of Hope Foundation, the Vince Carter Youth Basketball Academy, the annual Vince Carter Charity All Star Game, and the Nike Vince Carter Charity All-Star Golf Classic. In 2007, he received the Florida Governor's Point of Light award for his charity work in Florida, his home state.

- Like many professional athletes, retired Canadian synchronized swimmer and Olympic gold medal winner Michelle Cameron is involved in the Special Olympics. She also has interests in other children's charities, drug awareness programs, and preventative health and nutritional support programs.

The good name and reputation of professional athletes gather enthusiasm and resources for charitable activities.

Athletic teams often work together to raise funds for community causes. Here are a few examples:

- The MLB's Arizona Diamondbacks donate a lot of time and money to local organizations. In 2011, the team donated nearly $4 million to projects like renovating a new Boys and Girls Club and building a Vision Technology Center at a school for the blind. The team gives through the Arizona Diamondbacks Foundation, which has donated over $30 million since 1997.
- For two months in 2012, the Oakland Raiders NFL team donated 10 percent of all proceeds from season ticket sales to the Oakland school district. The total donation ended up being over $50,000.
- Basketball teams work together to promote NBA Cares, an organization that supports programs that make a difference. NBA cares builds basketball courts for kids, teaches about health and wellness, and promote a healthy environment. Players donate money and work on hands-on service projects.

According to the Character Counts Coalition, citizenship is:

- playing by the rules.
- obeying the law.
- doing your own share.
- respecting authority.
- keeping informed about current events.
- voting.
- protecting your neighbors and community.
- paying your taxes.
- giving to others in your community who are in need.
- volunteering to help.
- protecting the environment.
- conserving natural resources for the future.

The National Federation of State High School Associations believes that citizenship is a vital character trait for high school athletes. It defines these qualities as elements of citizenship:

1. **Perspective:** The ability to rationally recognize the relative importance of events in our lives and make sound judgments based on these priorities. Sports provide an opportunity to develop a healthy perspective on winning and losing and an ability to consider the place of sports in one's life.

2. **Sportsmanship:** Behavior that demonstrates playing by both the spirit and the letter of rules. The word "sportsmanship" is part of our general vocabulary because the values inherent in sportsmanship apply to relationships between people in many areas of endeavor. Coaches teach sportsmanship by what they say and what they do, and they can help athletes explore these values and develop sportsmanship skills.

3. **Teamwork:** The ability to work together to accomplish common goals. Teamwork is increasingly valued in business and in families, and can be learned through athletics when coaches intentionally develop and reinforce teamwork skills.

Like other professional sports organizations, the NFL is active in charitable giving. Many NFL players work in their communities to encourage youth to continue their education, to serve meals to the elderly with organizations such as Meals on Wheels, and to build homes for low-income families with organizations such as Habitat for Humanity. The "Hometown Huddle" is a national event that is conducted annually by the NFL in cooperation with the United Way. All 31 NFL teams participate in this coast-to-coast day of service. An estimated 300 and more players, family members, and other NFL representatives join forces with approximately 3000 representatives of United Way to lend assistance in a variety of ways to community members who are in need on this special day.

This admirable partnership began in 1973 when the United Way of America and the NFL first met to discuss the possible use of the NFL's network airtime to publicize and promote United Way and its activities during telecasts of football games. Pete Rozelle was the commissioner of the NFL at that time. Pete was well known for his understanding of *public relations*; he realized the value of a partnership like this one that would communicate the work of United Way while at the same time showing people who the players in the NFL really were. In this venue NFL athletes would have an opportunity to demonstrate aspects of their character that spectators don't have the opportunity to witness during a football game. Over the years this special partnership has shown itself to be a positive one for all concerned, perhaps most especially for the communities that have benefited from it. For over 35 years, this pairing of sports and thoughtful giving has stood as an example of what can happen when people and sports organizations come together for the greater good of their communities.

But you don't have to wait to be a sports professional to begin doing good in the world. You can start right now!

Few will have the greatness to bend history itself; but each of us can work to change a small portion of events, and in the total of all those acts will be written the history of this generation.

—Robert Kennedy

Track and field is just one sports opportunity you may want to consider.

CAREER OPPORTUNITIES

The field of sports offers many opportunities—and the chance to demonstrate a good character is one of the most important.

CHAPTER NINE

In the previous chapters, you discovered many interesting facts and stories about professional athletes and officials. By learning as much as you can about careers in the sports industry, you will better prepare yourself to make the important decision regarding what career is right for you. Whichever career you select, be assured that you will be presented with ample opportunities to show the world who you are. Your good character will go a long way toward building success in your chosen profession.

If you are dreaming of a career as a professional athlete, the time to start working toward success is right now. You'll need a realistic appreciation of the opportunities and challenges you might encounter in your chosen sport. In addition to playing whatever particular game you love, you need to be the kind of person who enjoys training your body. Most athletes must engage in weight training and aerobics as well as training specific to the skills necessary during game play. You want to enjoy all aspects of your chosen profession, and for a professional athlete that includes training. Often professional athletes must work more than 40 hours a week at least for the duration of the sporting season and often for most of the year. Would you enjoy spending more than 40 hours each week dedicating yourself to your chosen sport?

Irregular work hours are also a trademark of athletic careers, for athletes and coaches, referees, umpires, and other sports officials. Many sports are played on Saturday or Sunday, during the evenings, and even on holidays, including Thanksgiving and New Year's Day.

Most athletes, coaches, and sports officials spend a good deal of the playing season away from home. Do you think you would mind being separated from your family? This type of travel is often less

Employment Statistics

- There were 16,500 professional athletes in 2010, 242,900 coaches and scouts, and 19,500 sports officials like umpires and referees.

- Over half of all athletes (56 percent) work in spectator sports.

- Among coaches, 22 percent worked in elementary, middle, or high schools. Another 18 percent worked in colleges and universities.

- Most sports officials—29 percent—worked for the local government, 13 percent for spectator sports, and 11 percent at schools.

Umpires need to know the rules of their game.

enjoyable than other types because very little time is available for sight seeing, shopping, or eating in exciting restaurants. These are business trips, and in this case, they are all about practice and playing the sport.

Here's another question to ask yourself: Do you thrive on competition? This is a highly competitive business. If you are successful there will always be countless other players, or coaches, or even officials across the continent who would love to have your job. Even players on your own team may want to move up within the organization, so to a certain extent, your teammates may represent the competition. Or, you might not be a starter; you may be the player sitting on the bench hoping for an opportunity to replace your teammate.

If these considerations do not deter you from seriously considering your favorite sport you love as a career, do everything you can right now to find out all you can about this career. Here are some facts to get you started.

Jobs for athletes, coaches, umpires, and related workers are expected to increase about as fast as the average for all occupations

Canada has many professional lacrosse teams.

through the year 2020. Employment will grow as the public continues to increasingly participate in sports as a form of entertainment, recreation, and physical conditioning. Job growth will in part be driven by the growing numbers of *baby boomers* approaching retirement, where they are expected to become more active participants of leisure time activities such as golf and tennis that require instruction.

Opportunities will be best for coaches and instructors. A higher value is being placed upon physical fitness within our society, with Americans of all ages engaging in more physical fitness activities; they are taking part in amateur athletic competition, joining athletic clubs, and being encouraged to participate in physical education.

You may have noticed housing developments expanding in some suburban areas; where many houses are built, the need for a new school often follows. With new schools, the availability of new coaching positions grows. If you desire to become a high school coach remember these are usually part-time positions and teachers are often hired for them. Maybe you're thinking that what

Annual Earnings

Median annual earnings of athletes was $43,740 in 2010. The lowest 10 percent earned less than $17,120, and the top 10 percent earned more than $166,400 or more annually.

Median annual earnings of umpires and related workers were $22,840 in 2010. The lowest 10 percent earned less than $16,310, while the top 10 percent earned more than $50,350.

Median annual earnings of coaches and scouts were $28,340 in 2010. The lowest 10 percent earned less than $16,380, and the highest 10 percent earned more than $63,720. Median annual earnings in the industries employing the largest number of coaches and scouts in 2010 were as follows:

College, universities, and professional schools $39,750
Fitness and recreational sports centers $28,850
Other schools and institutions $25,150
Elementary and secondary schools $22,670
Civic and social organizations $21,150

you're interested in is coaching on the college level, but college coaches usually must build an impressive background in coaching at a lower level before any college will seriously consider hiring them. You may start as a high school coach, for example, and begin to get noticed by colleges after having several players develop the kinds of skills that impress college scouts or after having several championship seasons. If you apply for an assistant coaching position on a college team at that point, you may just get the job.

Competition for professional athlete jobs is expected to be intense in the years ahead. Employment will increase as new professional sports leagues are established and existing ones undergo

Professional boxing is another opportunity found in the world of sports.

expansion. Opportunities to make a living as a professional in individual sports such as golf, tennis, and others should increase as new tournaments are added and the prize money distributed to participants grows.

Since competition for jobs in professional athletics is so intense, put some serious thought into your backup plan. It is also wise to prepare for an alternate career along with your athletic activities because most athletes have a limited number of years that they can play a sport professionally. Whether they leave the sport because of injury, age, or just because they'd like to try something new, it pays to be prepared.

Opportunities should be favorable for persons seeking part-time umpire, referee, and other sports official jobs in high school level amateur sports. Job opportunities will be especially favorable for those working with women's sports teams. Competition, however, is expected for higher paying jobs at the college level, and even greater competition for jobs in professional sports. Earnings vary by education level, certification, and geographic region. Some instructors and coaches are paid a salary, while others may be paid by the hour, per session, or based on the number of participants.

Think about what you might want to do with your life if you are unable to become a professional athlete in the sport that you love. Would you want to have another type of job associated with the sport? There are many types of professionals who interact with athletes. Most professional athletes have an agent, for example. This is a person with a legal background who negotiates the athlete's team contract. They may also negotiate contracts for endorsements of products. A sports agent needs to possess significant knowledge of the game and excellent communication skills. Professional athletes may also have financial advisors and professional trainers. Perhaps you would be interested in a career in sports medicine or in play-by-play broadcasting. The knowledge of your sport that you are gaining now would be very valuable in any of these careers.

Sports is a career choice that more and more women are considering as well. According to the Women's Sports Foundation, there are over six million jobs in sport-related careers, a field that was once exclusively male. Over the past 30 years, barriers to the employment of women have diminished. Title IX of the 1972 Education Amendments Act (a federal law that prohibits discrimination against women in secondary and post-secondary educational institutions) eliminated quotas on the admission of women students to law, medical, and business schools, allowing women to get the educational credentials they needed to pursue their career interests in sports—from sports medicine to player agent/attorney.

Title IX also requires that women get the same chance as men to play varsity sports and opened the high school and college coaching and athletic management professions to women. In the 1970s, women were almost nonexistent in the sports media, where 99 percent of television hours and print column inches were devoted to men's sports. All that has changed today.

But some of the most important opportunities offered by a career in sports focus on character issues. As an athlete, coach, or sports official, you will have the chance to:

- demonstrate your integrity so that others will trust your leadership.
- show compassion and respect for others.
- be responsible enough that others will want to follow in your steps.
- live with justice and fairness, appreciating the unique value of each person.
- have the courage to stand up for what's right.
- be diligent and self-disciplined enough to stick to your career until you succeed.
- act on behalf of your community, demonstrating your citizenship.

Whatever you choose to do with your life, your life can make a difference.

All it takes is character.

Reputation is what you're perceived to be. Character is what you really are.

—John Wooden, UCLA coach

Further Reading

Buford, Kate. *Native American Son: The Life and Sporting Legend of Jim Thorpe.* New York: Alfred A. Knopf, 2012.

Dougherty, Jim and Brandon Castel. *Survival Guide for Coaching Youth Football.* Champaign, Ill.: Human Kinetics, 2010.

Josephson, Michael S. and Wes Hanson, editors. *The Power of Character.* Bloomington, Ind.: Unlimited Press, 2004.

Jones, Tom. *Working at the Ballpark.* New York: Skyhorse Publishing, 2008.

Kidder, Rushworth M. *How Good People Make Tough Choices.* New York: HarperCollins, 2009.

Thompson, Jim. *The Double-Goal Coach.* New York: HarperCollins, 2003.

For More Information

National High School Athletic Coaches Association
www.hscoaches.org

National Collegiate Athletic Association
www.ncaa.org

National Association of Sports Officials
www.naso.org

Center for the 4th and 5th Rs
www.cortland.edu/c4n5rs

Character Education Network
www.charactered.net

Josephson Institute of Ethics
www.josephsoninstitute.org

Publisher's Note:
The websites listed on this page were active at the time of publication. The publisher is not responsible for websites that have changed their address or discontinued operation since the date of publication. The publisher will review and update the websites upon each reprint.

Glossary

Baby boomers People born during the years of increased births after World War II.

Farm club A minor league baseball team that is subsidized by a major league.

Integrated Racially mixed.

Major league A league of the highest classification in U.S. professional baseball.

Minor league A professional sports league other than the major leagues.

Misconduct Inappropriate or unethical behavior.

No-hitter A game where the pitcher allows the opposing team no base hits.

Public relations Advertising; persuading the public to think well of an organization.

Segregated Racially separated.

Sportscaster A person who gives a radio or television broadcast of a sports event.

Index

About the Authors & Consultants

Joyce Libal is a graduate of the University of Wisconsin. She lives in northeastern Pennsylvania where she works as a magazine editor and freelance writer. She has also written books for other Mason Crest series, including Careers with Character and North American Folklore.

Rae Simons has written many novels and young adult nonfiction. She lives in New York State.

Ernestine G. Riggs is an associate professor at Loyola University Chicago. She has been involved in the field of education for more than forty years and has a diverse background in teaching and administration. Riggs was selected as one of the Outstanding Elementary Teachers of America by the United States Department of Defense Overseas Schools in 1974. She is the coauthor of *Beyond Rhetoric and Rainbows: A Journey to the Place Where Learning Lives, Helping Middle and High School Readers: Teaching and Learning Strategies Across the Curriculum*, and several journal articles. She is also co-featured in the video *Ensuring Success for "Low Yield" Students: Building Lives and Molding Futures*. In the summer of 2007, Riggs was invited to present a précis of the research on conation at the prestigious Oxford Round Table in Oxford, England. Riggs is a frequent presenter at local, district, national, and international conferences.

Cheryl R. Gholar has been a teacher, counselor, and administrator in public schools and worked in postsecondary education for more than thirty years. She is associate director of the Professional Development Consortium. Gholar is coauthor of *Beyond Rhetoric and Rainbows: A Journey to the Place Where Learning Lives*. She is also co-featured in the video *Ensuring Success for "Low Yield" Students: Building Lives and Molding Futures*. She is published in *Vitae Scholasticae, Black Issues in Higher Education, The Journal of Staff Development, Careers With Character*, and more. Gholar's awards include Educator of the Year; Phi Delta Kappa; Those Who Excel; Oppenheimer Family Foundation; Outstanding Teacher, Chicago Region PTA; and Outstanding Contributions to The Department of Character Education, Chicago Public Schools.

discard